The Short Cheap Tax Book for Multi-Level Marketing
50 things that every good MLM owner should do

Kirk Taylor, EA
Updated January of 2019

Copyright 2017-2019 Kirk Taylor

To the extent that the book uses specific numbers, they are for the 2018 tax year (returns being filed at the beginning of 2019). I will update periodically, but the book is designed such that you don't need to get a new copy every year (but it's cheap, so do it anyway, that way I know you love me!)

This is the second book in The Short Cheap Tax Book series.

These books are meant to expound upon the information on my blog: supertaxgenius.blogspot.com (Link #1) and in my other books in a targeted, specific and snarky way. My blog is meant for generic, public consumption at no charge. This book you pay for, so you get my very unvarnished, very uncensored opinions.

If you haven't figured it out by the title, this book is about Multi-Level Marketing (hereafter referred to as MLM). It will be most helpful to those truly trying to make real money, though anyone involved in one of these ventures can glean some useful information. Each chapter will be short and to the point, generally one page or less. Some of the information will be repetitive from the blog, but almost all will have expanded information and new perspectives, often initiated due to comments and questions I receive from the blog. A couple chapters are near direct copies from other of my books, because they are just too damn important to leave out, but will be modified as necessary to apply to an MLM owner. It will generally be ordered based on the importance I place on the subject, or a logical progression of ideas, or random: "I just don't know where to put this crapness."

This book will eventually be available as an audiobook (in theory) which is why each of the website links has a link number. If you are listening to this as an audiobook, you should have also downloaded a pdf file that has the links listed by chapter to allow you to click directly to the source, without having to type out the address while trying to listen. If you are reading this as an e-book, the link in the text will work directly by clicking on it. If you are reading a printed book, you will have to type the link into your browser, or do a search for it if the link is generic (such as the MileIQ link).

If you find this book useful, you should consider at least two of my other books. The Short Cheap Tax Book for Everyone (Link #2) and Everyday Taxes (Link #3). Make sure to get the latest year of Everyday Taxes. The first book has almost universally applicable great advice, and the second has dozens of chapters ordered around life events. The first is cheap, the second quite a bit more expensive because it has detailed information and takes months to write – so you're paying for the damage to my two typing fingers. That's right, everything in the books and on the blogs is written by a hunt and pecker.

DISCLAIMER:

Because lawyers suck and people are greedy, it's important to point out that this book represents MY opinions and interpretations, and are not necessarily those of the IRS or my employer. These chapters are short and sweet, so they don't cover all details and may not be accurate for your situation. Do your own research to be certain. Talk to a competent professional. Do not rely solely on this book. Also, client confidentiality is important, so the spirit of client stories is true, but the details are significantly altered.

Some Terms:

Since a lot of MLM companies try to disguise their nature, or make themselves seem "different" it's useful to define some of the terms I'm going to use:

MLM: A company that has people sell things but also encourages recruiting other people to sell the same things, from whom you get a cut of their sales. In some companies, the recruitment of a downline is the primary way to make money, in others selling is. In good ones, it's a nice balance.

Upline: The people above you who get a cut of your sales, and the sales of people below you. hey may be your advisors or supervisors.

Downline: The people below you, from whom you get a cut of their sales. You usually supervise the people you recruited, and maybe the recruits of the first group below them.

Sole Proprietorship: The most basic form of business entity, and the one that is assumed when you start a business. For these, you file the business taxes as part of your personal tax return, on a Schedule C. Unless otherwise discussed in a chapter, this book assumes you are a Sole Proprietorship (you can form a Limited Liability Company, and still file as a Sole Proprietorship – as long as you are the only owner.)

MLM Dilettante: Someone who participates in an MLM company primarily to get wholesale priced products for themselves or their friends, or to make just enough money to offset their purchases, such that they get their products "free". To the best of my knowledge, I invented this term. I should point out that, while I am not a lawyer, I suspect that this violates the law in some states.

Another Disclaimer: I will be ripping on MLM companies in general and by name for practices that I don't like. I'm not saying they are scams, or that you can't make money doing this, or that they're lying. I am saying that they are not tax professionals, and thus cannot be relied on for good tax advice. When I rip on one it is my OPINION with regard to what they are doing, based on information from my clients, and other sources (often their own web pages), and should not be interpreted as an indictment of the company, or the MLM business model. I have several highly successful MLM clients, and many more clients who are happy with their businesses, even if they aren't getting rich.

Now we begin the advice chapters. The first few are going to seem pretty obvious, but they are critical…

Print a Copy of Your Tax Return

If you have my first Short Cheap Tax Book, you might be a little worried since this is the first chapter in that book. Don't worry, it is included simply because it's that big of a deal.

What a stupid first page. I mean seriously, isn't this obvious? Based on how often I'm asked to get someone a copy of their tax return in the middle of summer, no, it's not. Print a copy, put it with all the supporting documents, and throw it in a safe place. I like one of those small, top opening file boxes. I keep stuffing them in until the new one doesn't fit, then I shred the oldest one. You should have 4 years at a minimum, but I probably have 7 to 10 years in there. While you're at it, if you can get an electronic copy, save that on your computer, and your backup hard drive, and maybe even a floppy disk (ask your parents if you don't know what that is). When you move, these files go with YOU, not in the moving van.

Make SURE that your tax pro gives you a copy. That ream of paper they give you is mostly crap, and often not the tax return. Many expect you to go home and print it out from some account they setup for you. I like the account idea, but make them print one anyway. You pay enough for tax prep that this is the least they can do.

This is especially important for a business. Each year, print a separate copy for the business and put it with all the receipts and records for that year.

Don't Lie to the IRS

Another every book chapter! Seriously, lying is a bad idea. Don't ignore them either. Exaggerate, stretch, manipulate, but don't lie. Two things the IRS hates more than anything: being lied to and being ignored. They're like your Mom.

I encourage taking the most aggressive tax position you can that's not a lie or frivolous. That said, if you get aggressive, you need to be prepared to lose in a fight with the IRS, just in case. Know how much money you're risking by being aggressive, and be prepared to pay some or all of it back at a later date. Odds are you'll get to keep the money, even if audited, but it's good to be prepared. Frivolous is loosely defined as a position that at less than one out of three tax experts would consider to be allowed.

For MLM companies, there are some areas of aggression that they just don't like. They don't like "training seminars" and conventions from your company (more details later). They don't like travel to visit family that is deducted as a business trip. They pay very close attention to conflating personal and business expenses. There are chapters on each of these things coming, so pay attention.

Get a Professional Tax Review Once in a While

Tax software and serious business people do not mix. Tax software sucks. It really does. It's designed to be user friendly, easy to use, and inexpensive. This does not result in accuracy. Odds are good that a good professional will find errors, and maybe even more money for you. That doesn't mean you have to pay for the review. Many tax pros will check your return for free, and then quote you a non-obligatory price for them to fix it. This is a win-win. Do it every three years at least. You get peace of mind, and maybe some money.

Try to find someone who handles a fair amount of MLM and/or retail sales businesses, but be careful of online advertised preparers who claim to be MLM "experts" and who promise great refunds or say that they won't miss deductions. These will get you in trouble.

I would also recommend a CPA or Enrolled Agent as the tax pro who does this review. You are much more likely to get great advice from them.

Don't Over Complicate your Records

Many people obsess about making sure every receipt is neatly categorized in perfect folder files, envelopes or fancy notebooks with pockets and stuff. They want to make sure that everything's perfectly ready for the IRS if they decide to audit them. This is all well and good, but it's probably not going to happen and you've wasted your time – time that could be sent SELLING! If this is how you want to do things, go for it, but make sure this doesn't keep you from writing everything down in an easy to use format.

For an MLM businesses, a good notebook or spreadsheet with all the expenses listed beats the hell out of a box of receipts, no matter how well organized. Save yourself some time. In the 1 in 100 chance the IRS wants to audit you, there's plenty of time to match the receipts to your notebook (and the notebook makes the IRS a lot more trusting if you're missing 1 or 2 receipts). Your time is far better spent growing your business or making it run more efficiently.

Have a mileage log or mileage app (discussed later).
Have a notebook for everything else. Have columns for date, description (make this a big column – have details), and amount paid or received.

That's it. Really. The reason I like this is that the notebook can always be with you. In the car, in your office, at a client's home, etc. This ensures that things get entered IMMEDIATELY! A spreadsheet or file system is great until it falls behind. The notebook is the easiest way to ensure this never happens. Feel free to convert to spreadsheets later if you want. A personal aside on spreadsheets: send the original spreadsheet files to your tax dude and not a pdf copy of them. While funny to watch, your tax dude trying to rearrange columns or do totals on a pdf is not very efficient.

Receipts go in a box or envelope, and we will only go after them if we need them for an audit.

Get a Separate Bank Account for the Business

I think this is a no brainer.

It doesn't have to be in the business name, just a separate account into which all income from the business goes. All expenses from the business come out of it except home office utilities, a non-business exclusive cell phone, and gas for the car (basically expenses that are not 100% business related). Estimated taxes and tax return balance dues will also be paid out of this account. Getting a debit card for the account is useful as well.

Having a separate account makes it very easy to back up your business expenses by showing a bank account register demonstrating them all. I also like it for assessing the relative success of the business. You also might eventually have to have the Hobby vs. Business discussion with the IRS, and this demonstrates profit motive seriousness.

Do NOT comingle business and personal accounts! The only time money moves between them is when you're transferring "profits" to your personal account to spend on personal stuff and (hopefully never) transferring personal funds due to a shortfall in income requiring an injection of funds. This shouldn't happen except very early in the life of the business. Keep good records when you do this, though it has no actual tax affect for a basic business structure.

Seriously – Do This!

Budgeting on a Variable Income

For starters, if this is a second income, upon which you won't have to rely for a while, follow the separate bank account advice from the previous chapter, and leave all the money, other than business expenses in the bank account until after you file your taxes. Pay your taxes out of the account, and then have your tax pro tell you what your net profit from the business was. This will be slightly suppressed due to some expenses you deduct not being "real" like mileage and office in home, but it's pretty accurate. Assuming you expect your business income to stay steady or go up for the next year (as it should) you can take that profit amount, multiply it by 0.75 and then divide it by 12. This is the amount you need to move from the business account to your personal account each month as a "salary". For a basic business model (not filing as partnership or corporation) there is no paperwork or tax implications of this. It is purely between you and the business. After filing taxes for the NEXT year, repeat the calculation and hopefully give yourself a raise. Any residual in the account after filing and paying taxes (and your first estimated payment if applicable) should be divided up between an amount of "bonus" you give yourself, business expansion expense, and a reserve for emergencies.

If you are making good money to start off, or can't afford to leave it all behind, you need to guess as to your minimum expected or lowest possible average month and use this as your withdrawal amount discussed above. Then repeat the calculations as each year when you file your taxes.

This system has several advantages, not the least of which is that it ensures you should always have enough money to pay your tax bill at the end of the year. This is because great months leave more money behind for taxes, and will cover for months where your income comes up short. This chapter avoids the necessity of setting aside income for taxes discussed in later chapters, as it does so automatically.

I have a later chapter about how much you are actually making that you can use for the calculations discussed above. Use the after-tax numbers that the calculation gives you, not the pre-tax numbers. I will do these calculations for you if I am your tax guy, and you can ask your guy or gal to do it for you as well.

Obviously, this chapter was about budgeting, and budgeting isn't just for personal income and expenses. Your business should have a budget of its own so that the business doesn't overspend, you can determine where changes can be made to improve profitability and you can figure out how much you are making and how it changes over time. All of this should be part of your business plan – we'll discuss this more in a later chapter.

Making Estimated Payments

I get asked about filing quarterly taxes all the time. What most people mean (even if they don't realize it) is making quarterly estimated tax payments. Only the more complex business structures file an actual quarterly tax return, small businesses just make estimated payments.

The IRS expects you to pay your taxes as you earn your income, so one way you can do it is to calculate an exact amount owed based on income and send it in every quarter. This is stupid. For one thing, it's an enormous waste of time – time that should be spent making money.

The IRS makes avoiding penalties for underpayment of taxes incredibly easy. My advice is to pay, in the form of estimated payments, EXACTLY what your tax liability was for the previous year (the tax return you filed Jan-Apr 2019 was for 2018, so 2019 estimated payments are based on this.) Your tax pro is a great way to figure this amount out, but, if you insist on doing your own taxes (another bad idea) you get the number from line 15 on Form 1040. You have to account for withholding from other jobs if you have them (or your spouses) which is easy assuming those incomes are steady. Just look at box 2 of the W-2's. For your first year, make NO estimated payments, and save money for taxes as advised in other chapters from this book. Take the tax liability and subtract the withholding from jobs from that. Divide this number by four, and send that amount in each quarter.

Estimated payments are due April 15th (yes, the same time your tax bill is due), June 15th (yes, only 2 months from the first – quarterly my butt), September 15th and January 15th of the following year. The exact dates may vary due to holidays, but will be no earlier than those dates.

If you follow this advice, and your business is growing, you WILL owe money at tax time. Follow the advice given in other chapters about saving money for taxes to make sure you have enough when you need it.

Save 30% for Taxes

If you don't follow the advice about bank accounts and budgeting from previous chapters, then you MUST save 30% of your GROSS (every dollar you take in) for taxes in order to be safe. This might not be enough (rarely) if you are in a higher tax bracket.

You pay taxes on your profit at a rate equal to your marginal tax rate (this is a stupid term for the tax bracket you are in) plus 15% (technically 15.3% on almost all your profit). You do get your deductions before the tax is calculated, but counting on them without doing serious math can be shaky. Seriously, do the budgeting and separate account stuff from earlier and this won't be a problem.

Now is a good time to explain that the extra 15.3% represents "self-employment tax" which is actually your Social Security and Medicare taxes. Every employee has 7.65% withheld from their pay to cover this, and their employer matches it. You pay both the employer's AND the employee's halves. For those bad at math, 7.65 time 2 equals 15.3.

You Might be a Hobby and Not a Business

The IRS is not going to allow you to just keep taking losses off of your regular income every year into the future. Some less reputable MLM companies love to recruit people by talking about tax deductions. I HATE the way Beach Body blathers about deducting your gym memberships and exercise equipment and getting a tax break. You probably heard that the IRS won't question your profit motive if you make a profit 3 out of every 5 years, and that's true, but not the important part of it.

I personally think that you should be busting your butt to make money, making changes when things don't work, and then evaluating where you are after three years and either quit, make BIG changes to generate a profit (or small changes if you're really close to profitability), or commit to the Hobby Model.

If the IRS questions the Business versus Hobby thing, there are a few things that will get you more attention. If you have another source of income that the business losses are helping you avoid paying taxes on, you will get a harder look. If your business records are in shambles, and you aren't behaving in a business-like manner, then things aren't looking good. If you keep doing the same things every year, and aren't making changes to try to reach profitability then you are in serious trouble. If you have a separate bank account, good records, make changes to increase profits, educate yourself on sales and good practices (NOT just through your company) and show increasing revenues every year (if not profit) you are doing the right things.

Working a good amount of hours, as if this was a real job (it is) helps a whole lot in this argument.

What if I AM a Hobby

Hobbies pay taxes on ALL their income, but don't pay the extra 15.3% self-employment taxes. The income is claimed on Line 21 of Schedule 1 of Form 1040 (other income).

Up until 2018, when the new tax law took effect, you were able to deduct expenses, but ONLY up to the amount of income you reported. They also got deducted as a part of itemized deductions, so if you didn't itemize, you got squat.

Starting with 2018, you have to include all of your income, and you get NO business deductions.

It's not a big deal if you have a few hundred dollars of income, but if you have thousands, being a Hobby is a BAD thing. For a lot of MLM dilettantes (someone who participates in an MLM company primarily to get wholesale priced products for themselves or their friends, or to make just enough money to offset their purchases, such that they get their products "free") this is actually the proper way to go, and should have minimal issues on their tax return. Think of any extra tax you pay as a "commission" on the low-priced or "free" stuff you get.

Before 2018 it could actually be harder to do a Hobby tax return than a business return, especially if you had a decent amount of money coming in and/or had a home office or used your car for the Hobby. You took deductions in a certain order, so as not to mess with other places where deductions went (if you own your home some of the Hobby expenses were already fully deductible on your itemized deductions.)

Hobby is easy now. You pay income taxes on all income, no extra self-employment taxes, and no deductions.

Understand How Your Company Reports Income

This is actually one of the hardest conversations I have at the tax desk.

Most new MLM clients have no idea what the numbers on their 1099MISC actually represent. The 1099MISC is how the company reports your gross income to you and to the IRS. In the modern world of MLM, where a lot of orders get handled by the company, and the "rep" (that's you) just makes the sale and enters it into the system for execution, there are a number of ways it might be handled. In the past, every penny that was collected from the customer, including the retail price, sales tax, and shipping was considered income for you. Nowadays, the company might only report your commission on the sale as income.

You MUST understand what they are reporting.

Good records where you track the sales you make, the shipping, sales tax and your commission can help a lot in figuring this out, but you should ASK, up front, how this works and insist that your upline, or a company rep explain EXACTLY how this is going to work.

This is very important because the reports the company provides have a lot of information, but you need to know how it translates to the tax return. If they report everything the customer pays as income to you, then you need to deduct the company's cut, shipping and sales tax. If they only report your commission, then you deduct very little regarding the sales. In this case, it's the cost of MAKING the sales that then becomes the big deal.

I'm going to be brutally honest. If you don't understand the flow of money in your business, and the way it's reported, much of this book is not going to be a lot of help. In addition, you will have difficulty getting your taxes done accurately, as well as understanding whether you are even making money.

Get a handle on this NOW!

Pay Attention to State and Local Rules…

…and taxes, and licenses, and file numbers and sales tax, and business personal property taxes, and inspections, and registrations and, and, and…

I'm not going to even TRY to cover all of these. I can barely keep up with my own state and tri-county area. I will say that sales tax is one of the REALLY BIG DEALS. Do not mess this up. People fear the IRS, but they should really fear the sales tax people.

Luckily, if your company manages shipping and payments, you probably have nothing to do on sales tax. If you personally sell items and collect money from clients, you need to know how to handle sales tax. Some states make it very easy, some not so much. Start with your state and county revenue department website. You should verify if you do or don't need a business license, and check on any other special taxes or regulations for your area.

Don't just rely on your upline for details on this. They were probably just as confused as you are mere months ago. A good place to start is a google search for, "starting a small business in SC". Use your state obviously. Scroll past any ads and prioritize results with a ".gov" ending. I get great information from the second result on that SC search:

http://www.sc.gov/business/Pages/STARTINGABUSINESS.aspx
(Link #4)

It's a link to a one-stop portal that takes you to almost everything you need. Not every state has this, and I guarantee it's not perfect, but it's a nice start. The best resource is to talk to a good local CPA with retail business experience, but that's not going to be cheap.

Don't Do It Just for The Tax Benefit

There are very few things that will improve your taxes without costing you in life. You only get a portion of that deduction off your taxes, so often times not paying something is better than getting the deduction.

People who tell you not to pay off your home mortgage because it's your best tax deduction are just stupid. You pay $10,000 in interest to get $2200 back on your taxes (based on the 22% tax bracket). BRILLIANT! You're out $7800! Now the tax benefit combined with other realities like you don't have $200,000 to pay the mortgage off or you have better things to do with the money can make this a smart idea, but don't just do it for the taxes.

This is especially important in business. Count how many times you hear your upline talk about "and it's a tax deduction!" This is CRAP! Paying money for the sake of a tax deduction is NOT a winning strategy!

Pay for things you have to, things that will make you more money, and things that will make the business run more efficiently (thus making you more money). Don't waste it on things that won't help.

Do You Need an Employer Identification Number?

Not right away, but you will eventually.

An Employer Identification Number (EIN) is basically the Social Security Number (SSN) for your business which means you don't have to give out your personal SSN. Before you get an EIN, the business operates under your SSN. This isn't a big deal, since you probably won't be giving it out to anyone other than your parent company, but, you might eventually need to change your business entity type, either for liability or tax purposes, and then you will definitely want to get an EIN.

If you get it right away, you might have to get a new EIN when you change business entity, which can be a pain (not getting the EIN, updating it with everybody using your old EIN). I would definitely wait to get an EIN until you are sure this is going to be a long-term prospect, you're sure what your business name will be, and you're sure that the business entity type is going to stay the same for a few years.

Deductible Business Expenses

The basic IRS requirement for deducting business expenses is that they be "ordinary and necessary".

I have my own definition for this: An expense is safely deductible if it is required by some authority, makes you more money, or makes the business run more efficiently. If it easily meets one of those requirements, it is almost certainly deductible unless it is something specifically not allowed, which we will discuss in later chapters. If you find yourself trying to twist things so they fit in those categories, you may be putting yourself at risk. When in doubt, ask a tax pro.

A few obvious examples: you are required to pay sales taxes, you have to have things to sell to make money, and a mileage tracking app makes the business run more efficiently.

Also, this book makes your business run more efficiently, and thus, is deductible.

The next few chapters will have some more details for you.

Entertainment

Primarily we're talking about picking up a meal or drinks for a current or a prospective client. The idea is that you have a reasonable expectation that the meeting might generate income for you now or in the future and that is the primary purpose of the meeting. You should write the name of the people you met, the purpose of the meeting and what was discussed on the receipt or in your log to be safe if audited. These meals should only include people who you are recruiting or attempting to sell to, and you should be VERY careful if you have a current social or family relationship with the person. Parties that are specifically for selling items and recruiting downlines are pretty much fully deductible, including food, drinks, prizes and host gifts. There's a lot of tax gobbledygook rules associated with this, but if you don't try to stretch the personal into the business, you will probably be safe.

The new tax law (starting in 2018) has all but eliminated entertainment expenses as a deduction, leaving only meals with clients or business associates as a deductible expense. This means that for parties, you may only be able to deduct the food. Essentially, everything that is fun, is not deductible.

Travel

We're talking about overnight travel here.

In order to deduct the expense, the primary purpose of the trip must be for business. There can be some personal time or entertainment, but it should be the minority of the time. If the primary purpose is business, you can deduct planes, trains, rental cars, mileage (if you drive your own car), taxis, hotel (actual costs), meals (you can use a federal daily per diem rate for the area instead of keeping receipts), tips and other related expenses. If the trip is not primarily for business, but you do some sales meetings, you can deduct the expenses directly related to the meetings in full, and ratio the rest of the expenses based on time spent on business activities.

If you go to visit friends or family, and try to turn it into a business trip, just don't. Unless you make some big sales or meet with non-family and friends to sell, don't deduct anything. If you do make sales via business meetings, deduct expenses in proportion to the time spent on business.

Travelling to training seminars and meetings hosted by your company are not something the IRS likes. They think these are rah-rah motivation meetings and not business meetings. If you attend these, you need to be prepared to provide documentation of the ways they were training you on how to grow your business and make more money.

Your Products

Okay, here's the deal: If you buy it to sell it, it's deductible (mostly - we'll talk about inventory next). What you pay for it, sales tax you remit, shipping and any other things you PAY to get it from your company and to your customer are deductible. You should be claiming the full amount you receive from the customer as income, and anything you pay out of that money is a deduction.

If you don't personally handle the sale, and instead get a commission or cut from the company, you need to know what they are reporting as income. If they report just the commission, you generally don't deduct anything, unless you have to pay something not handled by the company (such as shipping it to the customer from your house.)

If you buy product to physically demonstrate its use, or to show to customers during sales presentations, those would generally be deductible.

If you just use it to promote the product, such as wearing your company's product out and about, that is NOT deductible. That is personal use – this is not a close call so don't listen if your upline tells you something else.

If you both use things personally, AND use them in sales presentations (like a tube of makeup) you should also not be deducting it. In this case you should buy separately for personal use and business use.

Inventory

You don't need to read this section if your company handles the vast majority of your sales, such that the products very rarely pass through your hands, and the payments go directly to your company.

I used to hate inventory. It seemed like a whole lot of effort for not a lot of benefit. I've been changing my tune lately. The point of inventory is that you can't just buy a bunch of products at the end of the year to give you a ton of deductions to lower your income. In effect, you don't get to deduct the cost of something until you sell it. In reality, it's a lot simpler. You take your inventory (product on hand) at the beginning of the year (use what it cost you, though there are other ways), keep track of everything you buy to sell, as well as costs associated with getting or producing them (this is Cost of Goods Sold (COGS)), and then total up everything left at the end of the year (again using your cost). You also note anything withdrawn for personal use.

The nice thing about this is that it handles all the weird questions about personal use items, demonstration stuff, lost or broken products, returns etc. You don't need to get overly complicated with this, you just need to keep your product in an easy to inventory place, have a way of knowing what each item cost you, and a way of separating costs in your records that are part of COGS (I use an asterisk – no kidding). DON'T overthink this.

On December 31st, add up the cost of everything you have in inventory and that is the inventory number for your taxes. If you use a software program for tracking what you buy and sell, and what you still have on hand, it should be able to tell you what your inventory is. That said, you should reconcile it with inventory physically on hand each year, just to make sure.

You may be asked how you determine which of a number of identical items you have was the one sold or retained. You will hear about FIFO (first in, first out), LIFO (last in, first out) and others. Generally, this shouldn't be a big deal unless you have a lot of inventory. Usually you will just know which items you are talking about, and the costs stay the same, so you will be using the "specific identification method" meaning you know each item's cost individually and when it sells. If not use FIFO, which is pretty self-explanatory.

If this isn't obvious, your ending inventory from one year is the beginning inventory for the next. Beginning inventory in your first year is zero, and ending inventory in your last year of business needs to be zero (get rid of and/or account for all items that are no longer business related).

Depreciation

Big things you buy, with a life of longer than a year, like machinery, furniture, fixtures, or electronics often can't be deducted up front. You generally have to spread the deduction over several years.

But there's good news.

For an MLM business, relatively new de minimis rules (basically a fancy term for too small to be worth bothering with) will help ensure that you never have to depreciate anything (thank God – trust me on this). Any individual item you buy that costs less than $2500 can be deducted right away. The one downside to this is that if you buy something for the business, and later sell it, the entire proceeds of the sale are taxable as sale of business property – this is a pain. Basically, if you buy a camera for the business for $750 and deduct that cost, when you sell it, it is a sale of business property and everything you make on the sale is taxable, which isn't that big of a deal except the reporting can be confusing.

Talk to a pro if you buy anything for more than $2500, or sell anything used in the business other than your products.

You can bump that $2500 limit to $5000 if you do some paperwork. Talk to a pro if you are buying something between $2500 and $5000, they should be able to help and/or give you advice on what to do.

The only time you might see depreciation other than a purchase of more than $2500 is Office in Home deduction, which I will cover later.

Phones

If you only have one cell phone, don't try to deduct the purchase if you use it for personal use as well (you do – don't lie). You can deduct a reasonable percentage of the monthly bill, generally based on percent business use. There's no good way to get a perfect number, so my clients generally wing it based on their recollection.

What you pay for business features, separate business numbers or a second phone would be absolutely deductible. A home landline is generally only deducted to the extent you are deducting office in home (discussed later) but if you have a landline installed for the business (especially if you didn't have one before) you might be able to deduct it fully. In the modern cell phone world, a landline is weirdly more likely to be defensible as a business necessity than a personal necessity. Just make sure it is almost exclusively business use.

If you don't want to figure out a business use percentage, you could include it as a part of utilities in your home office calculation. We're talking about that next.

Home Office

You should have an area of your home that is regularly and EXCLUSIVELY used for business. This can be a standard office with a desk, a location for storage of business supplies and inventory, a place to meet customers, or a combination of all of these. It can be multiple places or one place. You need to know the square footage of the exclusive areas, and the entire home (your software or tax pro will want this.)

You can deduct home office in two different ways: $5 per square foot (up to 300 square feet) or you can ratio all household expenses based on the percentage of the house's square footage that is business use.

The $5 per square foot rule is designed to make things simpler, but most people take the method that gets better results. I think if it's close, or you aren't making a ton of money on your business, that you should take the $5 per square foot (especially if you own your home).

The regular method requires you to list all expenses for the home – rent, mortgage interest, taxes, insurance, repairs, utilities, pest control, warranties, HOA dues and more – and ratio them based on the square footage of the office area. This can get some great numbers! That said, if you own your home and use this method, you MUST depreciate the home and take a percentage of the depreciation as an office expense. This is not technically 100% true, but it is effectively so and is way too complicated to explain the differences here. This encumbers the home for sale in a confusing way – talk to a pro before using the regular method on a home you own.

Also realize that the mortgage and taxes are being partially deducted here, so only the remainder gets deducted in the usual, non-business place on Schedule A. Expenses directly related to the office areas can be deducted 100%. None of these office deductions can reduce your business income below zero. When you rent, the direct method often works out a lot better, and doesn't have any effect on selling your home, which is obvious since you don't own it anyway.

Office supplies such as paper, ink, pens, notebooks, staplers etc. are deductible as an office expense separate from home office if they are exclusively used for the business. Don't bother with business use percentages for most stuff that you use for personal and business such as ink and printer paper. Try to buy exclusively business use printers, laptops, staplers, supplies, etc. if your business warrants it. Separation of these expenses make things much simpler.

Legal and Professional Expenses

These are the basic expenses you pay to professionals for assistance in your business. Tax preparers, accountants, lawyers, advisors, search engine optimizers, programmers, designers etc. are all good examples. Also fees you pay to non-individuals such as legal zoom for business entity formation, legal documents and contracts also would apply.

This is a good time to mention that you shouldn't get worked up if you're not sure exactly what category things belong in on your return. Is the fee you pay to the county for a business license a tax, fee or a legal or professional expense? Who really cares? Just make sure you don't duplicate it in different categories.

When preparing taxes, I often like to indicate what line number of Schedule C (the business portion of your tax return) that I put various entries on, to make reconciliation easier if needed. I just annotate the line number next to the entry in the record of expenses, or write it on the receipt, or envelope of receipts. If your software doesn't tell you the line numbers (I hate that they do this) just write a simple list of categories, with a letter or number (your own personal code) that you write down to indicate where you entered it.

Excel spreadsheets are really awesome for this, but I still like starting with an extemporaneously written notebook where you write things down as they happen. In an excel spreadsheet I just add a column for the tax return line # and go through the whole spreadsheet indicating what everything is. Then I sort by that column and use excel magic to give me totals.

Advertising

Signs, paid web ads, newspaper ads, search engine optimizers, pretty much anything you pay to promote your business falls in this category. No, you can't put advertisements all over your car and make the car a business deduction, but you can deduct the cost of putting it on the car.

Along this line of thought, door magnets and stickers would be advertising. If you pay money for something that you reasonably believe will bring customers to your business, it's deductible even if it doesn't actually work. Just make sure you don't conflate personal and business, such as trying to deduct the whole car as discussed above, vice the decals.

Logo items such as mugs, stickers, t-shirts, etc. might be advertising, especially if you give them away. If you sell them, they're product, and go in inventory if you stock and sell them (or you just claim the income if you use a third party to produce and sell them for you). Obviously if you put them in inventory the income gets claimed as such when you sell them.

Random List of Things You Might Deduct

Most of the below assumes exclusive business use and is not exhaustive or guaranteed to be deductible. Mainly this is a brainstorming list for you.

Business cards
Logo items for customers
Professional publications
Books about selling/marketing/taxes/business management
Meals with prospective customers
Gifts to customers or vendors
Prizes
Car magnets
Stickers
Storage units for business supplies or inventory
Office equipment
Safe deposit box
Phone apps for the business
Mailing services
Email services
Premiums you pay to upgrade various things to business level (pro email, insurance riders, premium Linked-in access)
Display devices (tables, cases, cabinets)
Transport equipment such as boxes/suitcases/trunks
Booth rental for fairs or markets
Record keeping supplies
Contract labor
Advertising
Mileage
Office supplies
Professional services
Tax preparation
Phones and business lines
Commissions
Overnight travel
Professional organization dues
Training sessions
Sales education
Business software
Office software
Mail or email lists

Bookkeeping and accounting services
Licenses
Registration fees
Most taxes
Fees to establish business entities
Trademarks
Home office
Storage unit rental
Business equipment rental
Expenses exclusive to maintain your office space
Second phone number services (sideline/ring central)
Computers, laptops, tablets, printers or fax machines
Cameras
Product photography equipment
Vehicle expenses (unusual – you would generally be taking mileage)
Tolls
Parking
Car taxes
Demonstration products
Inventory
Business liability insurance
Business insurance riders
Workman's comp insurance.

Don't Believe What You Hear About Taxes

Unless you hear about it from a competent professional that you trust, it's very likely to be crap information.

Government websites are usually reliable.
Big financial publications (Kiplinger's for example) are pretty good.
Newspapers and broadcast news are terrible.
Blogs (other than mine), Facebook posts, friends, neighbors...all useless.

Competent tax professionals are the only people you should trust for sure. You can't even trust IRS employees. Believe it or not, if you get an answer from the IRS over the phone, if it's wrong, it's still on you. You need it in writing.

Your upline, your company and your co-workers might be the WORST source for tax information (or they might not). Many companies actively promote the tax deduction aspect of the business, and will encourage you to buy or participate in things that they charge you for, using "tax deduction" as one of the hooks.

Beware of Conflating Personal and Business

This is the BIG one.

The IRS audit guide practically ASSUMES that you are doing this. If you get audited, THIS will be something they will go after IMMEDIATELY!

Now that I've scared you, I'll remind you that the chances of an audit are slim. I tell you this not because I want you to ignore my advice on this subject, but because I HATE tax pros who use audit scare tactics. My rule: Never lie to the IRS, never ignore the IRS, but be as aggressive as your financial life will allow (you need to be financially prepared if the IRS does their worst).

Buying your own products for personal use, no matter how justified, is a non-starter. Trips that are primarily personal, such as visits to family, cannot be magically converted to business trips by making a few sales. Going to Vegas for a conference is okay only if the vast majority of your time is spent selling, marketing, learning and networking (not at the gaming tables or shows).

Your cell phone needs reasonable justification as to the extent of business use. Same for office equipment and furniture if not 100% business use (one printer in a household is not going to fly as 100% business use).

Some things are reasonably inexpensive enough that you should just spring for exclusive business use ones (printers, faxes, office supplies, small office equipment etc.) Other things, like computers or laptops, it can make sense to upgrade your system, and keep the old one, making one or another 100% business use.

Exercise equipment, gym memberships, personal grooming services and other things that normal people do, even if your reasons are based on your business are NOT deductible.

Don't Miss Mileage Deductions

Holy crap I LOVE Mileage!

This is oftentimes your best deduction!

Do not miss business related trips.

The IRS wants good records of this, starting with the total miles the car was driven for the year, so write the beginning and end odometer reading for the year. Your mileage log should have columns for: date, purpose of trip, and total trip miles at a minimum. Noting who you met with, if applicable, is helpful. A trip to the store to buy the mileage log is a business trip (unless you bought a bunch of non-business stuff as well). A trip to the grocery store to pick up refreshments for a party is deductible as long as most of the stuff was for the party.

The primary purpose of the trip needs to be business.

[MileIQ](#) (Link #5) provides a great app for tracking miles, for not a lot of money. It goes on your phone and you swipe for business or personal, then update the details. It's actually a little more work than a book, but it never forgets when the car was driven.

Mileage covers virtually every imaginable care expense, so you don't need to track gas, repairs, cleaning, or most other common expenses. You will track tolls, parking and taxes separately.

Don't Buy Every Promotional Package

First of all, some companies require you to make a certain number of sales, and a lot of MLM business owners make personal purchases to maintain their commission level or ability to buy wholesale. The fact that you "must" buy these doesn't make them deductible. They follow the same rules as everything else. If they are for personal use, they are not deductible. If you intend to sell them to someone, they become part of inventory. Only if they are immediately sold to customers, or used relatively soon as a demonstrator for customers are they deductible right away.

On a similar vein, promotional packages, kits or other things your company encourages you to buy should only be purchased if you are sure they will help you make more money or run the business better. They should NEVER be bought just because they are "deductible".

No matter how much you love your company, and no matter how much they promote their desire to help you be successful, it is critical to remember that they are in it for the money too. They are SELLING to YOU, just like YOU should be selling to EVERYONE.

Don't take everything they say, do or sell at face value.

Kids Can Sometimes Make Things Interesting

Sometimes it's better to make more money than less (for taxes only – in life it's always better to make more money). Kids are one area where this can be true, and extremely so. There are refundable tax credits that go UP as your income goes down, mainly the Earned Income Tax Credit (EITC).

I don't mention this so that you can use it to your advantage, but to let you know that you CANNOT fail to claim deductions simply because they improve your tax return. Having a business, and receiving some of these refundable tax credits creates a "due diligence" issue for tax pros. We can normally accept anything you say at close to face value, without being too suspicious, but EITC on a business tax return is cause for concern, and the IRS can hold us accountable for not being reasonably suspicious of things that don't add up, like door to door sales that don't have a mileage deduction, or a business with NO deductions, or a business loss that just "happens" to put the household at the perfect income to maximize EITC.

That said, there are legitimate ways to move income and deductions around, especially elections for Office in Home and depreciation, so a professional can definitely help. It can also be helpful to know that sometimes those shaky deductions that "might" be okay could be hurting you.

Bottom line, don't go crazy trying to maximize EITC, but don't ignore it either. Follow the basic Super Tax Genius rule of being honest and aggressive, but EITC might be an area to tone the aggression back, just a little bit.

Also make sure your records are solid if you find yourself getting some meaty EITC (the amount is on line 17a of Form 1040).

Random List of Things You Probably Can't Deduct

Some of the stuff on this list I'm including might be deductible for non MLM businesses or some weird MLM business I haven't heard of.

This list is specific to MLM.

No, Beach Body people, even YOU can't deduct gym memberships and exercise equipment.

Clothes
Items you use personally
Personal trips
Gym membership
Exercise equipment
Personal grooming
Haircuts
Forced purchases to meet quotas
Seminars that aren't educational in nature (rah-rah type seminars
Most car expenses if you use mileage
Personal use cell phone
A home office that isn't exclusive to the business
Meals for family and friends
Most expenses that are "fun"
Items that are not ordinary and necessary for your business

Accounting Method? WTF and Why Do I Care?

Your accounting method is the cash method.

You have other options, and sometimes you are not allowed to use the cash method, but trust me, cash is the way it is until you change business entity or make a whole crap ton of money (millions).

Your accounting period is a calendar year. Again, it doesn't have to be, but it is for you.

You mainly care about this because your tax pro or software will ask, and you need to know what year to put things on your tax return.

This is all about what year your income and expenses are counted in. If you get the money in 2019, it goes on your 2019 tax return. If you spend money in 2019, it goes on your 2019 tax return. A few examples to make things clearer…

If you get a check in 2019, it goes on 2019, even if you don't, or couldn't cash it in 2019.

You include expenses in the year you pay them, unless they are for a different year. The main one you'll see this for are insurance policies. If you pay for one year of liability insurance on October 1st of 2019, you only deduct 3 months in 2019 and 9 months in 2020. If you pay for things with a credit card, the date paid is the date you swiped the card, not the date you pay the bill, however if you are invoiced for a service, you deduct it on the date you send the check or otherwise pay the bill, not the date you get the invoice.

You can't intentionally move income into a later year by asking someone to delay payment.

Let's Talk About Liability

Liability is basically you being responsible for bad things that happen as a result of your business. Say, someone burns themselves while cooking at a Pampered Chef party or someone has an allergic reaction to your Avon lipstick and now looks like Mick Jagger.

In our lawyer centric society, you could be held responsible for these things.

Now this is a tax book, so I can't give you great advice on what to do, but you need to know that, at least initially, everything you own is on the hook if you get sued and lose big. EVERYTHING. You need to think about the risks you face, what your current insurance will cover, and what you can do to prevent issues. Business liability insurance (or a homeowner's insurance business rider) or forming a limited liability company are two ways to protect yourself.

Don't assume that just because you deal mostly with friends that you are protected – and – as I'm going to point out repeatedly later – you aren't going to make real money just selling to friends and family.

Have an Emergency Fund

This isn't really about taxes, except that a big tax bill is an emergency that would make having an emergency fund nice, and a tax refund is often the easiest way to start an emergency fund. Your emergency fund should be 3 to 6 months of living expenses.

The cool thing about having one, is that this dude named Murphy, who has a law named after him, keeps track of who does and who doesn't have an emergency fund. Emergencies happen to people without an emergency fund, and generally don't happen to people who are prepared to handle them.

You should have an emergency fund for your family and another one for your business. You don't want to be scrambling for money when you have an unexpected business expense. In the beginning, set aside some personal money to get the business started, and try to make sure it's the right amount, so you aren't constantly robbing from the personal money to keep the business afloat. Once income is rolling in, a good amount needs to be retained for future expenses, emergencies or business slow periods.

What About Partnerships

I am not a fan of partnerships.
At least not equal ones.
Someone needs to be the boss.
Someone needs to have the final say.

That said, there are a lot of reasons you might form a partnership, but that's not what this chapter is about. This chapter is about accidently forming a partnership without meaning to. If two or more persons work together on a business, sharing expenses and income, that's a partnership, even if it wasn't your intention to file Form 1065 Partnership Tax Return and issue K-1's to each partner with their share of the business profit or loss.

If you want to work with someone in your business, get a CPA involved to learn all the various ways you can do it, and the positives and negatives of each. Then, draw up a real partnership agreement or other applicable business entity laying out all aspects of the venture, making sure to cover all positive and negative potential outcomes. You should probably get lawyers involved in this. Don't just shake hands and hope everything will work out – it won't.

The exception to this is spouses. Spouses can work together on a business and each file a Schedule C with their share of the business income and expenses. A Schedule C just goes on your personal tax return, and doesn't require a fancy separate business return. I'm not a huge fan of this either, but it's not that big of a deal.

Extension Misconceptions

An extension is an extension of time to FILE, not time to PAY.

The extension gets you out of the failure to file penalty, but not the failure to pay penalty. You are expected to pay what you will owe with the extension, which requires at least some attempt at preparing a return.

Wandering into a tax office to file an extension on the last day of tax season with no documents in hand is practically a waste of time. An extension is better than nothing, but take some time in March to get at least SOME of your income information in to your tax dude or tax software.

If you KNOW that you are due a refund, you don't need an extension. If this is the case, and you will be filing by October, don't bother with the extension, there is no penalty if the IRS owes YOU money.

I added this chapter from the first book to explain that having an MLM business is not an excuse to file an extension. If your records aren't up-to-date enough to file taxes on time, then you're doing it wrong. Also, if your tax person extends you every year, even if you've provided all paperwork in a timely manner (timely means by mid-March), then he or she is overworked and probably not giving you the attention you deserve.

Buying Stuff for Yourself

Items that you buy for personal use are not deductible.

You can't justify it by saying that you have to "advertise" it, or demonstrate that you love it.

This doesn't work.

You can get sneaky with some stuff like jewelry by wearing it, hoping someone will see it and want to buy it, and eventually selling it, but you need to have inventory in order to do this. While you are wearing it, the item remains in inventory, effectively not being deducted.

Don't push this.

If, like many people, you are only doing this to get products you like at wholesale, and do very little selling, or recruiting of downlines, you are what I call an MLM Dilettante. In this case it's not a business and you don't get to take a loss. The Gross Income goes on Line 21 of Schedule 1 as Other Income (not subject to self-employment taxes) and you don't get to deduct any expenses (prior to 2018 your expenses were a miscellaneous itemized deduction). You are required to claim income you make even if your company doesn't issue you a 1099MISC. I know no one does this, but that's the law.

There's a chapter in this book with more details on being a Hobby vice a business.

Retirement

I'm not going to spend a lot of time on this, because it's way too complicated for a short, cheap book, but there are some things you should know.

If this is your sole source of income, then the major source of most people's retirement savings, a 401k plan through your employer, is not available to you. In addition, your Social Security contributions are based on your self-employment tax (based on net income) so you may be under contributing, thus limiting how much you might get when you retire. You can still contribute to Roth or Traditional IRA's, but your contribution is limited by your NET PROFIT from your business.

If you are living on your business income then there's probably plenty of money to maximize your contributions, but it might not.

You can also form a Simplified Employee Pension (SEP) Plan, which has much higher limits. This will require assistance from a financial advisor.

Bottom line is that you need a plan for retirement. A good financial advisor can be extremely helpful.

Even if this isn't your sole source of income, you should consider how it affects your retirement plans because the SEP is still a great way to save for retirement.

Talk to a pro.

Health Insurance

I am not a Health Insurance expert, but, there are some things you should know about Health Insurance.

One, up through 2018, you were required to have health insurance or face a penalty. The penalty could be up to 2.5% of your income.

If you do get insurance privately (even if it's through the Obamacare website), the premiums you pay out of pocket might be deductible. If you have no other insurance available (if it's available but you decline it then you can't deduct premiums) then you can probably deduct the premiums you pay out of pocket. If you get a subsidy through Obamacare you figure the deduction amount after reconciling the subsidy with your income on your tax return.

This deduction does not come off the business, but does come off on the front page of the 1040, meaning you don't have to itemize to get it. In other words, it saves you on income taxes (based on your tax bracket) but not the extra 15.3% self-employment tax you pay to cover Social Security and Medicare.

If you get a premium subsidy through the ACA, then things get complicated. Your subsidy is based on your household income as reported on your most recent tax return, and updated as you tell them your income changes. When you file your taxes, they calculate the ACTUAL subsidy you should have gotten, and either take some back (subject to some limitations based on income) or give you more. It's important to note that your business income counts towards this, but only after you deduct business expenses. Based on this, if you are making more money this year than last, you need to update the exchange so your subsidy can be lowered.

You also need to have a little extra money set aside for taxes, just in case things get ugly. If your income goes above 4 times the poverty level, you have to pay back EVERY PENNY of your subsidy!

How Much Am I Really Making

There are many reasons you might want to know how much money you are making, but sometimes the answer is not easy to find.

One of the reasons is to calculate a salary for budgeting, others would be for determining if the business is worth continuing, figuring your hourly income, or for selling the business.

All of the methods below have limitations and inaccuracies, the more common causes being:
1. Numbers that are based on IRS allowed values such as mileage or meals
2. Things that become deductible that you would have paid anyway, like the home office
3. Taxes from another job or income source, like your spouse(spouse)
4. Things you pay up front but that the IRS makes you wait to deduct such as depreciation or inventory).

The methods that follow are designed to get you cash flow type numbers vice a number based on some accounting method (Generally Accepted Accounting Principles (GAAP) is the CPA speak for this).

The easiest and most accurate way (if you are scrupulous with your business account) is to use the separate bank account I discussed before, and take the balance just after filing and paying your taxes in the current year, subtract the amount from the prior year just after paying taxes, and add all "salary" withdrawals you made. This method takes taxes into account. If you want pre-tax income, just add back any estimated or actual taxes paid.

The other method would be to take line 28 of your schedule C and make adjustments based on the following lines (your tax pro can help with this):
Line 9: Either add back the entire amount on this line, or a percentage based on how expensive your car is to operate (based on repairs and gas mileage). If you don't drive your car a lot for business, add the whole thing back. If you use actual vehicle expenses vice mileage, don't do anything with this line.
Line 13: Add this line back to line 28 and then subtract the total you paid for depreciable property in the year in question (the numbers should be on a depreciation schedule with your tax return.)

Line 24b: Add this entire line back, and estimate what you paid ONLY for meals another person ate.

This number does not take taxes into account. If you want after taxes, subtract estimates paid and actual taxes owed when filing.

Some Thoughts on Your Downline

We're entering an area of the book where the advice is less about taxes, and more about business. I will focus as much as possible on the tax side of things, but some things I've picked up from doing taxes for a lot of MLM businesses are worth passing on. Take them with a grain of salt, and understand you can't blame me if the advice sucks.

For many MLM professionals, the downline is where they make all their money. Choose aggressive, smart and capable people, but recognize, the more shared friends you have, the more they will be competing with you for business. Also recognize that the income they generate for you will have very few deductions, so will be heavily taxed.

This is a GOOD thing!

Downlines generate money with little cost or effort on your part after initial training. Just be aware of this as tax time approaches.

Nurture your downline until you are sure they are ready to be successful on their own. They are an investment in future income for yourself.

Don't waste effort on people who won't put the effort in or who aren't making progress.

If You Don't Hate Tax Time…

You're not doing it right

Actually, if you follow all of my advice, and are being successful, and making lots of money, tax time should suck, but in a sort of good way. You should be pissed that you are writing a big check to the government, but you shouldn't be wondering where the money will come from. It should already be set aside, ready to go. The frustration should be that you don't get to keep all of it, just some of it. You should be happy that we are able to increase your "salary" due to you having a higher profit. You should be mad that your estimated payments have to go up.

If you are getting a big refund, something isn't going right, and you should challenge yourself to make next year suck big time!

Credit

I am very anti borrowing money.

This is a personal thing, but it clouds my advice. I will say that borrowing money to expand your business is a bad idea unless you have a clear plan for how it will translate into increased income, a plan to pay it back, and it is not tied to any personal assets. This means no Home Equity Loans or Mortgages. To put it in a Dave Ramsey-ish way: Are you willing to lose your home if your business fails?

To be honest, I can't really convince myself that there's a good reason for an MLM company to borrow money – sorry.

Read the IRS Tax Audit Guide

The one for Retail Trade previously had some great insights into how the IRS feels about MLM companies. Much of my scary, don't do this stuff came from the previous audit guide. Unfortunately, it's being revised and is currently unavailable. Figures that they would do it right when I'm writing a book on MLM taxes, but that's Murphy for you.

The link below is for the previous audit guide from 2009. Keep checking back and download and read the new one when it becomes available again:

https://www.irs.gov/pub/irs-mssp/retail_industry_audit_technique-guide.pdf (Link #6)

Epic anti-IRS rant warning:

I wrote the first edition of this book in 2017. It is now 2019. The audit guide revision is STILL not done! How the hell long does it take to revise one fricking document!

Most People Lose Money

Just have to say it.

Very few people who get into these types of businesses make any money at all. The ones that do are the ones who treat it like a business or job, working dozens of hours a week minimum, and are hustling and learning to try to make things better. Despite anything else you've heard, this is not a simple or easy way to make money without expending a lot of effort.

I'm not trying to tell you not to do it, I'm telling you to manage your expectations, and make sure to have a plan. Too many people just dump money and time in, without a clear idea if it's working, or if the business is going anywhere.

Work. Every day. Lots of hours. Have a plan.

Work.

What is Your Audit Risk?

People LOVE worrying about audits, and warning you about audits.

Your chance of a face to face audit is almost negligible. Negligible.

A correspondence audit, on the other hand, is also very rare, but somewhat more likely (and easier). A correspondence audit is one where they ask you for documentation related to a specific deduction or credit, or a category of deductions.

Your most likely type of "audit" is a CP2000 letter, usually caused by you failing to include some piece of income or tax information on your return that was reported to the IRS. The risk of this is directly proportional to how careful you are making sure you get and report all the paperwork you should have. The 1099MISC and/or 1099K are the big ones you want to make sure are reported on your return (the Gross Income line from Schedule C (Line 1) should equal or exceed the total of those forms unless you have a good reason).

Don't worry about audits.

Make sure you are doing things right, keeping good records, and not lying.

You should be okay.

It's All About Sales!

If you can't sell, you can't win at this.

You need to sell yourself, the company and the products at every opportunity. You need to love what you do and love what you sell. If you don't, you're just wasting your time. You need to practice your pitch and your delivery. You need to build the confidence to talk to anyone, anytime and try to make a sale. This is true about many things in life. Almost everyone is a salesman in one way or another, and the ones who recognize this and work to get better are the ones who are succeeding.

Get out and find some sales skills! Your upline "should" be your best place for this, but you also need to get and read books, review sales blogs and articles and cultivate friends and acquaintances who are successful salespeople.

A lot of your expenses in this area, especially books and training will be deductible.

Face to Face is How You Sell

Other than referrals from current clients, most of my new tax clients come from face to face interactions, usually at a bar. Bars are a place where people are relatively comfortable talking to strangers, at least most of them are – especially in the South. That said, don't just run around to bars getting drunk as your primary recruiting tool, but don't miss any interaction where you could get a sale.

I don't do MLM – no time or inclination – but one of the biggest complaints I air to my MLM clients is that they don't even ATTEMPT to recruit me. They don't need to be pushy, but they should at least ask, and ALWAYS ask to leave some business cards. I'm pretty sure if they don't ask me, they're not asking enough people. You need to approach at least 100 people for every successful sale you make that's not to family and friends, and you will NEVER win just selling to family and friends. Get used to hearing "no" and be polite and unoffended when you are rejected, even though you shouldn't always accept no right away.

EVERY interaction is a sales opportunity – barber, car salesman, pet groomer, mechanic, strangers in lines, tax dude, friends of friends, other salespeople, contractors, plumbers, cashiers, and more!

Hone Your Sales Skills

"Hi, I'm Bob, would you like to buy some stuff?" is a terrible way to sell.

While everyone who sells stuff should have a 30 second "elevator pitch" it's often better to ease things into the area of sales. You need to master this, and get used to rejection. Practice with family and friends, and work until your sales pitch is natural and fluid. Don't be a pain, but also don't roll over at the first sign of rejection. It's helpful to know what the prospective client's interests are before you start selling, so you can tailor your approach to fit them.

Your upline should walk you through some sales presentations, and should allow you to do some attempts under their instruction, all while giving you good pointers as you work. If your direct upline isn't a lot of use then try to find the person above THEM who is the king or queen of sales.

If you were totally sucked in by the person who recruited you, and you found the opportunity compelling and hard to resist, then you have found the right person to work with. MAKE them teach you. It's their JOB. They get a cut of everything you sell so they OWE you training and time.

Get better at this, take some classes, read some books. Network with people who kick ass!

Consider Making a Business Plan

Most MLM owners never even think about a business plan.

Why?

Successful businesses almost always have one. A business plan lets you put all aspects of the business in one place. It forces you to think about HOW you are going to make money.

A good business plan will include benchmarks, expected expenses in detail (called a budget), marketing plans, cash flow expectations, and many other aspects that should be considered. I'm not an expert on these, but I've seen some good ones. Take some time, think about what the business should look like going forward. Jot notes down on what you think is going to happen and when. Be holistic and general at first, imagining how things will happen. Make a nice general outline based on this and then continue narrowing it down with details, numbers and plans.

Pretty soon you'll have a good idea of what needs to happen, how it's going to happen, how much time it will take and how much it's going to cost. You will also have an idea how the business is going to grow, and how you are going to meet your long-term income goals.

There are a lot of great books and websites that can help you with this. A little planning now goes a long way to making you successful later.

Tax Software Sucks

Why does tax software suck?

Simple: it has to be both user friendly, easy to use, and accurate. If it's not user friendly and easy to use, no one's going to pay for it. Hell, that's why it's so popular! It is simply not possible to cover all the complexities of tax law and business taxes and still be easy to use. So, they make it easy to use: "How much did you pay for uniforms?" Sure, there's an info button you can click that will go into all the nitty gritty of this question, but if you read them every time they come up, it's not simple and easy anymore. "How many miles did you drive for business last year?" Again, many pop-ups will be available to help you navigate the dizzying rules that are involved in this simple question, but you're not likely to read them, and, if you do, they're only going to make you more confused. Don't even get me started on depreciation, business use of home, or investing income!

And that's just the Federal return!

Many states have nearly incomprehensible tax laws, and dozens of deductions and credits that you pretty much need to know exist in order to take advantage of them. Most software just drags things from the Federal to the State, with barely a peep about what deductions you might miss.

I cannot even begin to describe the messes I've seen from tax software. Just recently, a client with one W-2, no wife, no kids, no house, and an amazingly simple Federal 1040EZ missed out on over $10,000 in state tax money over the last dozen years because either the software didn't ask, or he neglected to answer enough questions, to establish that his military income was exempt from California taxes. Most of that money is gone forever.

Tax preparation software SUCKS!

You will have a better chance at an accurate return using pen and paper with the Federal and State instructions than you will using software!

This is especially true with MLM companies.

The New 20% Business Deduction

The next three paragraphs will cover the changes for the vast majority of people. The rest is for people making a lot of money (relatively speaking).

This has been called the "pass-through" deduction, but that's not really accurate. It includes almost all business income, including sole-proprietorships, S corporations, limited liability companies and income from investments in publicly traded partnerships and real estate investment trusts. It definitely applies to the standard MLM business.

There are a lot of weird provisions that kick in above a certain income, but if your TAXABLE income is less than $157,500 ($315,000 Married Filing Jointly), then this pretty much applies to all business income and you get to deduct 20% of your net profit from each business directly off of your taxable income. This is designed to cause all businesses to pay about the same tax rate as corporations do with the new lower corporate rate. The deduction does NOT reduce your self-employment tax, meaning the extra 15-ish percent you pay for Social security and Medicare.

This rule is very unusual in that you have to do your tax return all the way through just before figuring your tax, and THEN apply this deduction. It uses taxable income for virtually all tests and calculations, as opposed to Gross or Adjusted Gross Income like almost everything else in the tax world.

Above those numbers, a lot of weirdness kicks in.

If your business is service oriented and your taxable income is over $157,500 ($315,000 MFJ), then your deduction starts to phase out and will be completely gone at $207,500 ($415,000 MFJ). An MLM business is not likely to be service oriented, so you can ignore this unless you provide services instead of a product. Service oriented means the primary thing you are selling is your knowledge and ability, as opposed to a physical product or labor.

If your taxable income is $157,500 ($315,000 MFJ) and you have a non-service business, then the deduction is up to 20% of business income, but subject to a limitation based on wages or depreciable property in service that also phases in such that the limit fully applies at taxable income of $207,500 ($415,000 MFJ). Chances are very good that if you exceed this income, you will not have any of the items discussed below that allow you to take the deduction, simply by the nature of an MLM business.

The wage limitation when fully phased in applies such that the most you can deduct is the greater of 50% of W-2 wages paid by the company (including your own wages) or 25% of W-2 wages plus 2.5% of the original basis of all qualified property. See an expert if this applies to you.

This is an over-simplified explanation. If there's a chance this applies to you beyond very small dollar amounts, suck it up and pay a really good professional for help this year.

There is No 1040EZ or 1040A Anymore

Just the Form 1040.

In an effort to deliver on the promise of a simplified tax form that could be filed as a postcard (not that you ever would, of course) the Form 1040 was modified to put all of the most common items on one half page form, and move all the rest of the stuff to six schedules.

So now, the base 1040 is the only form, and you use schedules as necessary.

To be clear, nothing is simpler than it was before, just moved around.

www.ingramcontent.com/pod-product-compliance
Lightning Source LLC
Chambersburg PA
CBHW050020230526
45470CB00003B/1049